Did You Know?
BRIGHTON & HOVE
A MISCELLANY

Compiled by Julia Skinner

With particular reference to the work of Helen Livingston

THE FRANCIS FRITH COLLECTION

www.francisfrith.com

Based on a book first published in the United Kingdom in 2005 by The Francis Frith Collection®

This edition published exclusively for Bradwell Books in 2013
For trade enquiries see: www.bradwellbooks.com or tel: 0800 834 920
ISBN 978-1-84589-441-2

British Library Cataloguing in Publication Data

Did You Know? Brighton & Hove - A Miscellany
Compiled by Julia Skinner
With particular reference to the work of Helen Livingston

The Francis Frith Collection
6 Oakley Business Park,
Wylye Road, Dinton,
Wiltshire SP3 5EU
Tel: +44 (0) 1722 716 376
Email: info@francisfrith.co.uk
www.francisfrith.com

Printed and bound in Malaysia
Contains material sourced from responsibly managed forests

Front Cover: **HOVE, THE PARADE 1921** 71501p

The colour-tinting is for illustrative purposes only, and is not intended to be historically accurate

CONTENTS

2 Introduction

4 Sussex Dialect Words and Phrases

5 Haunted Brighton & Hove

6 Brighton & Hove Miscellany

43 Sporting Brighton & Hove

44 Quiz Questions

46 Recipes

48 Quiz Answers

54 Francis Frith - Pioneer Victorian Photographer

INTRODUCTION

'But have we any leisure for a description of Brighton? … for Brighton, that always looks brisk, gay and gaudy, like a harlequin's jacket … for Brighton, which used to be seven hours distant from London … which is now only a hundred minutes off.'
(William Thackeray, 'Vanity Fair', 1847.)

Busy, breezy 'Doctor Brighton', where the crowds came to take the waters and be dipped in the sea, was the first Sussex resort town to develop into a popular Georgian watering place during the late 18th century. Brighton was originally a small fishing village called Brighthelmstone, but when Dr Richard Russell moved there in 1754 to supervise his sea water cures, for glandular diseases in particular, he publicised the resort. Dr Russell recommended not only sea bathing but also that sea water should be drunk, hot with a little milk or cream of tartar, an idea that, amazingly, caught on with fashionable society. Brighton soon gained a reputation as a centre of fun, frivolity and fashion, an image enhanced by the patronage of the Prince Regent, who made his first visit to Brighton in 1783 at the age of 21 and was delighted with the place. The prince - later George IV - secretly (and illegally) married the Roman Catholic Maria Fitzherbert in 1785, who lived in a villa at Brighton; in order to be near her he took a lease on a 'superior farmhouse', and Brighton's success was assured.

The opening of the London to Brighton Railway in 1841 rapidly changed Brighton from a watering place for fashionable society into a centre of mass entertainment. The famous 'Brighton Belle', which ran until the late 1960s, could do the journey from London in 55 minutes. Brighton became popular not only for long periods of recreation but also short holidays and as a destination for day-trippers, as well as acquiring a rather risqué reputation as a resort for an illicit break - 'the Brighton weekend'. The Metropole Hotel on the seafront, which opened in 1890, soon became a mecca for fashionable society, the 'London set', reaching a zenith in Edwardian times. Brighton's population rapidly increased, from 45,000 in 1841 to over 120,000 by 1900, and it developed into the biggest and liveliest of the Sussex resorts.

Hove developed from a number of hamlets to the west of Brighton. The waters of St Anne's Well, a chalybeate spring, were recommended by Dr Russell in his treatise of the 1750s which helped to make Brighton popular, and Hove grew in the wake of its neighbour. Brunswick Terrace, perhaps the most magnificent Regency development in Britain, was completed in 1830, and further seafront terraces and squares followed.

Although Brighton and Hove have now been amalgamated into a city, in the past Hove was a much quieter and more conservative town than its neighbour, and deliberately provided fewer mass entertainment facilities than Brighton.

Brighton boomed between the wars of the 20th century; by the mid 1930s it was packed at weekends. After the Second World War, Brighton and other Sussex towns were still popular for holidays, but in the 1960s the popularity of package holidays took the tourists abroad. However, the position of Brighton & Hove within commuting distance of London has given the area a sophisticated, cosmopolitan feel, and it is sometimes referred to as 'London by the Sea'; the lively atmosphere is enhanced by the presence of students at the various higher education establishments in the area, as well as a number of foreign language schools. Today, although the holiday trade is falling off, Brighton & Hove is a popular conference venue, and the marina, built in the 1970s to provide moorings for 2,000 boats, has given the seafront a new lease of life.

SUSSEX DIALECT WORDS AND PHRASES

'Windogs' - clouds blown across the sky by a strong wind.

'Knuckerhole' - a spring which rises in the South Downs.

'Squatelings' - female conversation or chatter.

'Twitten' - a narrow path between hedges.

'Loving mud' - sticky mud.

'Outlandish' - foreign, out of the local neighbourhood.

'Looker' - a shepherd.

'Slummocky' - messy, untidy.

'Swimey' - feeling sick or faint.

'You may push and you may shov
But I'm hemmed if I'll be druv
... For Sussex will be Sussex, and Sussex won't be druv.'

HAUNTED BRIGHTON & HOVE

Brighton & Hove can claim to be one of the most haunted places in the country, and one of the best ways to learn about the local ghost stories is to go on one of the organised Ghost Walks that are available. Here is a small selection of the ghostly locations in the area:

A famous Brighton ghost is that of a woman dressed in grey who haunts Meeting House Lane, disappearing through an arch which was bricked up in the mid 19th century. Tradition says that she is the ghost of a nun who was walled up alive here in medieval times after running away with her lover, but another theory is that she may have been a Quaker, as Quaker women also dressed in sober colours.

North of The Dials is the Port Hall area, which takes its name from the unusual 19th-century Port Hall, said to be haunted by the ghost of a crusader dressed in red.

White Hawke Hill was once the site of White Hawk Fair, which was held there for a few years from 1791. Ethel Elmore, the daughter of the squire of Woodingdean, disappeared after visiting the fair and was said to haunt the area - sightings were reported of a ghostly woman in a pure white gown, which became known as the White Hawk Lady. The ghost was not seen any more after a female skeleton was found in 1807, which was assumed to be that of Ethel.

The 200-year-old Bedford Tavern in Western Street, just off the seafront on the border between Brighton and Hove, is famous for a number of resident ghosts.

A touching tale from medieval times is that of Lady Edona, who waited in St Nicholas's churchyard for her lover, Manfred de Warrenne, to return from the Crusades. Sadly, as she watched, his ship sank just offshore at Brighton and he was drowned. Legend says that a ghostly ship, St Nicholas's Galley, can be seen gliding into Brighton at midnight on 17 May each year.

BRIGHTON & HOVE MISCELLANY

Thomas Brock's superb 13ft-high bronze statue of Queen Victoria, which stands at the seaward end of Hove's Grand Avenue, was unveiled in 1901 (see photograph 48507, opposite). It was designed to commemorate the 60th anniversary of Queen Victoria's accession, but she died before the statue was completed and the unveiling was a very subdued affair.

After the Norman Conquest King William ordered a great survey to be made of the wealth of his newly won territory in 1086, which came to be known as the Domesday Book. In this survey the settlement at Brighton was called Bristemestune, and an annual rent of 4,000 herring was established.

St Nicholas's Church is the oldest building in Brighton. Various theories have been put forward to explain why the church was built on a hill: perhaps it was sited here to be away from coastal erosion, or to be at a safe distance from attack by the French, but the most likely explanation is that fires could be lit on the flat church tower which would act as a beacon to fishermen and sailors. This theory is supported by the fact that St Nicholas is the patron saint of seafarers. The church is noteworthy for its beautiful Norman font, dating from about 1160, which is carved with religious scenes such as the baptism of Christ, the Last Supper and the legend of St Nicholas.

HOVE, THE VICTORIA STATUE
1902 48507

BRIGHTON, THE CHAIN PIER 1870 B208003

Piers were originally jetties for boats and ships to moor beyond the low tide mark, but they soon evolved into pleasure zones in their own right, and assumed exotic architectural styles. Brighton's Chain Pier of 1823 was the first pleasure pier ever to be built, and both Constable and Turner were inspired to paint it. Designed by Captain Samuel Brown, the Chain Pier was like a four-span suspension bridge, jutting about 1,000ft into the sea (see photographs B208003, above, and B2085017 on page 49). Sadly, this historic structure was swept away in a storm in 1896.

Fossilised remains of prehistoric creatures such as mammoths, woolly rhinoceri, hippopotami and primitive horses have been found in caves below Black Rock.

Brighton obviously had a slightly risqué reputation in Jane Austen's day. In 'Pride and Prejudice', Elizabeth Bennett begs her father not to allow her younger sister Lydia to go to Brighton, aware that she will be easily led astray by the company she will meet there. Her father ignores the advice, and the result is the scandal of Lydia's elopement with Wickham.

The 1896 storm that destroyed the Chain Pier also badly damaged the West Pier, as can be seen in photograph B2085009, below.

BRIGHTON, WEST PIER c1896 B2085009

During the 'Fashionable Season' between October and January, the rich and famous would 'promenade' by the sea and on the pier in the mornings, and then spend the afternoon driving along the seafront drives of Marine Parade and King's Road from Kemp Town to Brunswick Town. In order to protect the prestigious dwellings of Marine Parade, a great sea wall was built along the cliff in the 1830s, and a road was constructed along it. This was immediately fashionable with 'promenaders' because of its sheltered location and its proximity to the Chain Pier. It was rebuilt as Madeira Drive (known as Madeira Road until the First World War), and improved in the 1890s with the building of Madeira Terrace raised on its graceful cast iron arches; the Madeira Lift carried people from Madeira Drive to Marine Parade.

BRIGHTON, MARINE PARADE 1921 71499

BRIGHTON, WEST PIER PAVILION FROM KING'S ROAD 1894 33763

West Pier was designed by Eugenius Birch in his Turkish-exotic style, and opened in 1866. By 1894 it had been extensively rebuilt (but Birch's entry kiosk survives), and a landing stage for paddle steamers had been added, together with a new pavilion. Paddle steamers had been introduced as a visitor attraction in the 1880s, after their initial function had been superseded by the railways.

The writer and traveller Daniel Defoe visited Brighton in the early 18th century and made the following comment: 'The sea is very unkind ... (and the inhabitants) might reasonably expect it would eat up the whole town, above one hundred houses having been devoured by the water in a few years past.'

The 'Anglo-Saxon Chronicle' contains the first mention of a settlement in the Brighton area; its name was recorded as Beorthelm's-tun, meaning 'the town of Beorthelm'.

The West Pier, seen in all its glory in photograph 48495, below, was enlarged at the seaward end in 1890 to accommodate a larger pavilion. This pier has been sadly derelict for many years, and despite being taken over by a Trust and gaining Lottery funding for its restoration, objections, storms and arson damage appear to have sealed the fate of Eugenius Birch's masterpiece.

BRIGHTON, THE WEST PIER 1902 48495

The steeply-cliffed nature of Brighton's eastern seafront from Rottingdean to the Palace Pier gives it quite a different flavour than the seafront to the west. The beach lies well below the main cliff-top road, and was originally the ladies' bathing beach. Ladies would enter the water from bathing machines licensed by Brighton Corporation. They cost 9 pence per half-hour (6 pence for gentlemen). There were 150 ladies' machines and 100 gentlemen's in 1880. Mixed bathing was finally sanctioned by the Corporation in 1901, and then only from bathing machines. 79 years later the world was changed indeed, when Brighton became the first major resort in the country to sanction a naturist beach - at Cliff bathing beach below Duke's Mound.

The sign on the clock tower in photograph B2085008, opposite, reminiscent of Nelson's message before the battle of Trafalgar in 1805, reflects the wartime date of the photograph. Brighton's position on the south coast made it vulnerable during the Second World War; 198 people were killed in air raids on the town, nearly 800 people were injured, and over 2,000 houses were destroyed.

One of the treasures in the Hove Museum and Art Gallery in New Church Road is the Hove amber cup. This was found in an oak coffin in a long-barrow grave at Hove in 1857, along with a stone axe-head and a bronze dagger, and the bones of the deceased. The cup is nearly 7cm (3 inches) high, and was turned on a lathe from a single block of Baltic amber.

ENGLAND
STILL
EXPECTS
YOU
TO DO YOUR
DUTY.

BRIGHTON, THE ROYAL PAVILION 1889 22244

BRIGHTON, SEAFRONT HOTELS 1890 27609

The astonishing building known as the Royal Pavilion at Brighton started life as a farmhouse, and then became a Classical villa with a rotunda before John Nash (the architect of London's Regent's Park) transformed it for the Prince Regent (later George IV) into the romantic domed and minareted Indian-Moghul-style palace, seen in photograph 22244, opposite. The design of the Royal Pavilion may have been the inspiration for the architects who designed so many 19th-century piers, bandstands and seafront shelters around the country in a hybrid of Moorish-Indian-Arabic style. At a time when many people did not travel abroad, before cinema and television, exotic buildings were known only by engravings and later by photographs and magic lantern shows, so the impact of these unusual structures was an important factor in attracting visitors to seaside resorts. In 1846 Parliament voted to sell the Pavilion; fortunately the town bought it, and it remains Brighton's fantastical centrepiece, attracting thousands of visitors every year. Inside, the 18th-century 'chinoiserie' décor has been beautifully preserved, and the kitchens, where the celebrated chef Careme reigned, are of particular interest.

Photograph 27609, opposite, shows two of Brighton's famous seafront hotels: on the left is the red brick Metropole, designed by Alfred Waterhouse, which opened in the year this photograph was taken, and on the right is the Grand. The Grand was built in 1862-64 in the Italianate style. It was severely damaged by a terrorist bomb during the Conservative Party Conference in 1984, but has been restored to its former glory.

Brighton's Palace Pier was designed by R St Moore, and opened in 1899, proudly proclaimed as 'the finest pier in the world'. An exotic hybrid of Turkish-Oriental-Arabic style was selected, and the pier offered everything its Victorian visitors could desire, on 1,760ft

BRIGHTON, THE PALACE PIER 1902 48513

of promenade deck with ornate domes and glass-covered sun verandas. The theatre at the end of the pier was added in 1901. Many of the slot-machines and other amusements that delighted Edwardian visitors are still in use.

BRIGHTON, GOAT CARTS 1889 22238x

Goat carts were available for children to hire in Brighton from the 1830s - they were expensive, costing one shilling per hour by the mid 19th century. Several goat carts can be seen in photograph 22238x, opposite.

Fashionable Victorian society at Brighton was summed up thus by Richard Jefferies (1848-1887): 'It is a Piccadilly crowd by the sea - exactly the same style of people you meet in Piccadilly, but freer in dress, and particularly in hats. All fashionable Brighton parades the King's Road twice a day, morning and afternoon, always on the side of the shops. The route is up and down the King's Road as far as Preston Street, back again and up East Street. Riding and driving Brighton extends its Rotten Row sometimes to Third Avenue, Hove. These well-dressed and leading people never look at the sea. Watching by the gold-plate shop you will not observe a single glance in the direction of the sea, beautiful as it is, gleaming under the sunlight. They do not take the slightest interest in sea, or sun, or sky, or the fresh breezes calling white horses from the deep. Their pursuits are purely 'social', and neither ladies nor gentlemen ever go on the beach or lie where the surf comes to the feet. The beach is ignored; it is almost, perhaps, quite vulgar; or rather it is entirely outside the pale. No one rows, very few sail; the sea is not 'the thing' in Brighton, which is the least nautical of seaside places. There is more talk of horses.'

The late Dusty Springfield and her brother Tom once lived in Wilbury Road, Hove. They formed a group known as The Springfields before Dusty went solo to become one of the most popular female singers of the 1960s.

Brighton's parish church, St Peter's, was built in the 1820s at Richmond Green, just north of The Steine, and designated as the parish church in 1873. It was designed by Charles Barry, who was later knighted for his work as the architect of the Houses of Parliament, and was originally a chapel-of-ease to the old parish church of St Nicholas, set up on the hill to the west.

In August 1862 the Brighton Gazette reported on an unusual wedding that took place at St Nicholas's Church. The bride was Sarah Forbes Bonetta, who was a West African princess who had been orphaned at an early age after a massacre, and abducted by a neighbouring tribe. In 1850, two years after her capture, the young girl was seen by Commander Forbes from England, who was visiting King Gezo of Dahomia in West Africa as part of negotiations to try and stop the African slave trade. King Gezo gave the child to Forbes to take back to England as a 'gift' for Queen Victoria, and Forbes named her Sarah Forbes Bonetta ('Bonetta' was the name of the ship they sailed on). Queen Victoria took a great liking to the child, and arranged for Mrs Forbes to educate her. In 1862 Sarah married an African American man, John Davies, in Brighton. The Brighton Gazette reported that the guests included 'white ladies with African gentlemen, and African ladies with white gentlemen until all the space was filled. The bridesmaids were 16 in number'. Sarah and John had three children, the eldest of whom was Queen Victoria's goddaughter. When Sarah died in 1880, the queen wrote in her diary: 'Saw poor Victoria Davies, my black godchild, who learnt this morning of the death of her dear mother'.

BRIGHTON, THE OLD STEINE 1902 48522

Once marshy ground used for drying fishing nets, The Steine at Brighton was drained and turned into elegant gardens. Surrounded by fashionable tall lodging houses, it provided an alternative promenade to the windy seafront.

Old Brighton was a fishing village bounded by West Street, East Street and North Street, that area of town now known as 'The Lanes' which is such a favourite with tourists. There was once a South Street, and indeed a whole 'lower town' on the beach, but they were both claimed by the sea in the early 18th century.

Brighton acquired the first public electric railway in 1883 when Magnus Volk's seafront line opened. It originally ran from the Aquarium to the Chain Pier, and extended east to Kemp Town's Paston Place in 1884. It still runs along the seashore in summer, between Black Rock and Brighton Pier.

St Margaret's Church at Rottingdean stands on the site of a Saxon predecessor (see photograph 22255, below). It was burned by the French in 1377, along with Rottingdean's inhabitants, who had taken shelter inside it. Even today, burn marks are still visible.

ROTTINGDEAN, THE CHURCH
1889 22255

After Magnus Volk's Electric Railway on the seafront was licensed in 1883, the Corporation eventually followed suit with its own electric tram system. Photograph B208002, below, shows tram

lines being laid along North Street from Grand Parade. Brighton's extensive tram network was completed in 1904, and ran until just before the Second World War.

BRIGHTON, LAYING TRAM LINES IN NORTH ROAD c1904 B208002

ROTTINGDEAN, THE WINDMILL c1965 R62037

A hundred years ago, windmills were a ubiquitous feature of the downland landscape of Sussex. Rottingdean windmill looks rather decrepit and forlorn today, stranded in the middle of the golf course (see photograph R62037, opposite). Legend has it that this famous smock mill never actually ground corn but was used by smugglers for signalling.

Phoebe Hessel is one of the most remarkable characters in the story of Brighton & Hove. She was born in 1713 and joined the army disguised as a man, a deceit which she carried out successfully for several years. Phoebe was in love with a soldier called Samuel Golding, and enlisted to be able to stay with him when he was posted to the West Indies. When her lover was wounded and invalided out Phoebe had no reason to stay in the army and revealed her sex to the commanding officer, after which she was discharged. After Samuel Golding died, Phoebe moved to Brighton where she married William Hessel. He died when she was 80, and Phoebe received three guineas from the parish. She used this money to buy a donkey and became a well-known character in Brighton, hawking fish and other goods such as gingerbread and apples. In 1808 Phoebe received a pension from the Prince Regent of half a guinea a week, and when he became George IV she attended his coronation in 1821. She lived to the remarkable age of 108 and is buried in St Nicholas's churchyard.

The electorate of the Brighton & Hove area seem to be considerably more concerned about environmental issues than in the rest of the country. In the 2005 general election, the Green Party took 22% of the vote of the Brighton Pavilion constituency, against just 1% nationally.

Hove has some particularly fine churches. The old parish church of St Andrew, which today nestles incongruously under the town gasometer, dates back to medieval times, but it became ruinous during the 18th century and was entirely rebuilt in 1836. All Saint's Church, built at the end of the 19th century, is a superbly grand affair. St Leonard's, Aldrington, went up in the 1870s, and the Church of St John the Baptist, which was built in Palmeira Square in 1852 to serve the Adelaide Crescent development, adds an elegance with its soaring spire of about 1870 (see photograph 41897, opposite).

In 1896 the first London to Brighton motor race was organised to mark the passing into law of the Locomotives on the Highway Act, which meant light locomotives could travel 10mph faster than they ever had before. The new speed limit was now 14mph, and the law abolished the need for a man to walk in front of the car waving a red flag. Lord Winchelsea symbolically destroyed a red flag at the start of the first race, which was called the Emancipation Run, as a demonstration that the motor-car was here to stay. The London to Brighton Veteran Car Run is still held today, and showcases the reliability of the cars that were made before 1905. Held in November, it attracts car enthusiasts and celebrities from all over the world. At the centenary celebrations of the rally in 1996, three cars from the original run were among the 660 cars which took part. The race was started by Lord Winchelsea, the great-grandson of the first starter, who tore up another red flag to signal the off.

HOVE, THE CHURCH OF ST JOHN THE BAPTIST
1898 41897

BRIGHTON, THE DEVIL'S DYKE 1902 48527

The Devil's Dyke near Brighton has long been a popular destination
for visitors and offers long views across the Weald of Sussex - see
photograph 48527, above. The Dyke was said to have been dug
by the Devil. He was so infuriated by the Christian piety of Sussex
people that he began to dig the Dyke in the hope that the sea would
rush through to flood the Weald and drown them. His plot was foiled
by an old woman who rushed up the hill with a lighted candle held
behind a sieve, which fooled a cockerel into thinking it was dawn.
Hearing the cockerel crow, the Devil abandoned his task and fled, for
he cannot bear sunlight. To the left of the flagpole in the photograph,
a pier of the Dyke cable car can be seen. This vertigo-inducing ride,
which stretched across the valley, lasted from 1894 to 1907; the
places where the pier stood are still visible.

Always jealous of its independence in the 19th century, Hove evaded Brighton's dominance and obtained borough status in 1898. Alfred Waterhouse, later the architect of Brighton's splendid Metropole Hotel, designed an impressive red brick and terracotta Town Hall in 1882, shown in photograph 41896, below. Its imposing tower held a carillion of twelve bells, which played a different tune for every day of the week. Sadly, Waterhouse's Town Hall burnt down in 1966 and a modern structure took its place.

When the first London to Brighton motor race was held in 1896, the organisers' instructions revealed: 'Owners and drivers should remember that motor-cars are on trial in England and that any rashness or carelessness might injure the industry in this country'. Of the 33 cars that began the first run only 14 completed it, although there were rumours that one car was fiendishly brought down by train and covered in mud before the crossing line.

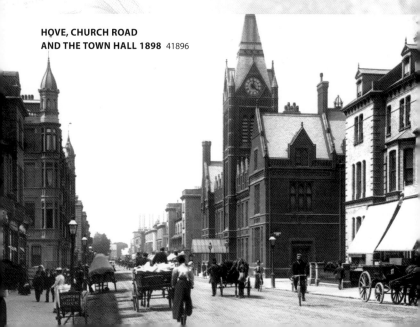

HOVE, CHURCH ROAD AND THE TOWN HALL 1898 41896

Hove, originally a small fishing village west of Brighton, developed slowly from the mid 19th century onwards. As at Brighton, large areas of working class housing arose away from the sea front. The Drive, seen in photograph 41895, below, is typical of the

HOVE, THE DRIVE 1898 41895

development of the Stanford Estate after 1871: yellow brick semi-detached villas with cement dressings, slate roofs and bay windows in wide tree-lined streets - totally different from Hove's earlier grand stucco terraces, seen in photograph 71501 on page 41.

BRIGHTON, THE 'SKYLARK' SETS SAIL 1902 48504

'All aboard the Skylark!' During the 19th and early 20th
centuries there was a great vogue for boat trips from the
beach; many former fishing vessels were thus employed,
notably the 'Skylark' (see photograph 48504, above), a boat that
became so famous that 'Skylark' became a generic term for the
pleasure boats of Brighton.

Beach donkeys were a feature of Brighton's seafront until the Second
World War. They plied the lower esplanade with their youthful
mounts, since the pebbly beach made it impossible for them to
be ridden there. Dark rumours hung around these donkeys in the
mid 19th century, for they were reputed to be used by the local
smugglers to carry contraband spirits.

Brighton Station, terminus of the London, Brighton and South Coast Railway, was designed by David Mocatta and opened in 1841. David Mocatta was a student of Sir John Soane, and reputedly helped in the construction of the Bank of England building in London. As well as the original façade of Brighton railway station (although this is now difficult to see because of later additions), Mocatta also designed the Italianate pavilions on the Ouse viaduct near Haywards Heath. The Brighton & Hove Bus Company commemorates him - it is part of company policy to name their fleet vehicles after historical figures who have figured prominently in Brighton's development.

Brighton's municipal camping ground, seen in photograph B208510 below, which opened in 1938, was the first such campsite in the country. It was situated in the Sheepcote Valley, between the racecourse and Black Rock, incorporating the former Newhouse Farm. It closed in the early 1990s.

BRIGHTON, SHEEPCOTE VALLEY MUNICIPAL CAMPING GROUND
c1955 B208510

ROTTINGDEAN, THE VILLAGE c1965 R62081

To the east of Brighton is Rottingdean, a coastal village sheltering in a little combe. Photograph R62081, above, shows the village pond at Rottingdean, which was once popular with downland shepherds. During the Victorian period many artists and writers were drawn to live in Rottingdean by the tranquil atmosphere of the village, the most famous of whom were Sir Edward Burne-Jones and Rudyard Kipling; the Downs around Rottingdean inspired Kipling's poem 'Sussex', which summed up the landscape in a single line: 'Our blunt, bow-headed, whale-backed Downs.'

Built into the wall surrounding Rudyard Kipling's old house at Rottingdean is a lucky stone head. Local legend says that anyone who strokes the nose gently in a clockwise motion with the forefinger of the right hand and then turns around three times will be granted their dearest wish.

The Dome at the Royal Pavilion, once the Prince Regent's stables and riding school, has now been divided into a concert hall and exhibition centre and the Brighton Museum and Art Gallery. Amongst the exhibits to be found in the Museum and Art Gallery, which has a lively and fast growing collection of 20th-century decorative arts, are brilliant examples of Lalique glass, as well as an important costume collection, and a fascinating exhibition depicting local history.

The seedy underworld of Brighton in the 1930s and 1940s was explored by Graham Green in his novel 'Brighton Rock'. The book is a dark tale of gangs and murder, and reaches an exciting climax at the Kemp Town racecourse. The book was turned into a film in 1947, in which the vicious Brighton gangster Pinkie Brown was played by Richard Attenborough.

BRIGHTON, THE ROYAL PAVILION, THE DOME 1902 48524

During the First World War, troops from the Indian Army fought on the Western Front. Several buildings in Brighton were employed as hospitals for wounded Indian soldiers, including Brighton General Hospital (which was renamed the Kitchener General Indian Hospital), the York Place school, and the Royal Pavilion. Provision had to be made to accommodate places of worship for the three main religions of the Indian troops (for instance, a marquee was erected as the Sikh temple) and nine kitchens were erected in the grounds of the Royal Pavilion to cater for all the different dietary needs of the various religions of the soldiers.

The Bat and Ball pub in Ditchling Road takes its name from the old Sussex game of Bat and Trap, which was played on The Level opposite. The pub has two signs, and the picture on the sign in Ditchling Road depicts the 'correct' game referred to in the pub's name. The other sign, showing a cricketer, is a reminder of the time in the 1980s when the pub's name was changed to Lords Bar and given an erroneous cricketing connection. Bat and trap is a very old game, which was traditionally played on The Level on Good Friday morning. The ball is thrown into the air by the trap, a seesaw-like catapult, when the batsman hits the raised end of the trap with his bat.

The BBC and ITV sports commentator Des Lynam started his career at BBC Radio Brighton.

HOVE, THE PARADE 1921 71501

During the 1960s Brighton was the scene of several clashes between rival youth culture gangs known as the 'mods' and the 'rockers'. The worse clash was on 17-18 May 1964, when 3,000 youths fought in the town. The incident was made the subject of a feature film, 'Quadrophenia', in 1979, much of which was filmed on location in the city. The name comes from the album 'Quadrophenia' by The Who; this now-legendary supergroup was the resident band in The Florida Rooms in Brighton in the 1960s.

St Nicholas's churchyard was the burial place of several famous names in Brighton & Hove's history such as Martha Gunn, 'queen of the dippers' (the attendants who looked after women bathers in the 18th century), Phoebe Hessel, who had disguised herself as a man to fight in the British army alongside her lover (see more information on page 29), and Captain Nicholas Tattersell, who took Charles II to safety across the English Channel after the battle of Worcester in 1651.

BRIGHTON, WEST PIER AND THE BOATING LAKE 1925 78309

BRIGHTON, THE PARADE 1894 33719

SPORTING BRIGHTON & HOVE

Chris Eubank is surely the area's most charismatic sporting character. Eubank adopted Brighton as his home, and it was from here that he launched his glittering boxing career. After a long unbroken run of professional wins, Eubank won the WBC World Middleweight title in 1990, and then successfully defended it twice. Apart from his wonderful ability in the ring Eubank is almost as well known for his somewhat eccentric personality. He is an elaborate dresser, who twice won Britain's 'Best Dressed Man' award, and he is also noted for driving unusual vehicles around town, including an enormous truck!

The county cricket ground at Hove is one of the country's more interesting cricket venues. Little more than a stone's throw from the sea, the area was formerly a barley field, and was re-laid as a cricket ground in 1872. The proximity to the sea is often thought to have a marked impact on the playing conditions, and it has been said that the pitch's characteristics differ depending on the state of the tide. The sea fret, or misty conditions coming off the sea, certainly does regularly affect play by assisting the bowling side. The permanent floodlights, amongst the first in the country, are another notable feature of the ground.

Steve Ovett must lay claim to being the most successful Brighton-born sportsman. A world-class middle distance runner, Ovett set two world 1500-metre records, and in 1980 won Olympic Gold in the 800-metre event at the Moscow Games. The 800-metre victory was something of a surprise, since Ovett's great rival Sebastian Coe was expected to win the event. A few days later Ovett surprisingly lost the 1500-metre Olympic final, but he remains one of the sport's all time greats.

Brighton and Hove Albion FC has always retained loyal support as Sussex's only League club. Although the club has never really achieved great success in the game, the loyalty of its supporters remains constant. For instance, the club had a remarkable average attendance of more than 18,000 in the Division Four championship-winning season of 1964-5. Fans are currently anticipating the building of a new stadium for the club at Falmer - permission was granted for this in October 2005.

QUIZ QUESTIONS

Answers on page 48.

1. Which king is King's Road named after?

2. The Booth Museum of Natural History in Dyke Road has a collection of nearly half a million varieties of … what?

3. What was described by William Cobbett (1763-1835) as a combination of 'a square box, a large Norfolk turnip and four onions'?

4. What is the link between Brighton and the recipe for Tournedos Rossini which is on page 47?

5. The great actor Sir Laurence Olivier made his first professional theatrical appearance in a sketch at the Brighton Hippodrome in 1924. However, he would not have viewed this moment as one of his greatest triumphs on the stage - what happened?

6. What is the connection between Brighton and Alice in Wonderland?

7. Where in Brighton can you see a stone sculpture of the Loaves and Fishes parable from the Bible, when Jesus miraculously fed 5,000 people?

8. What important event occurred for Brighton and Hove in the year 2000?

9. Every February an event known as 'Seedy Sunday' takes place at the Old Market in Hove - what is this event about?

10. The Station pub next to the railway station at Hove was once known by another name, possibly the longest pub name in history - what was it, and what is the story behind it?

RECIPE

BRIGHTON ROCKS

Ingredients

225g/8oz plain flour
100g/4oz butter or margarine
100g/4oz caster sugar

2 beaten eggs
50g/2oz currants
50g/2oz ground almonds
1 teaspoon lemon juice

Cream the fat and the sugar in a bowl. Save one teaspoon of beaten egg and beat the rest into the mixture, then add in the lemon juice. Mix in the currants, ground almonds and flour.

Form the mixture into small balls and place them on greased baking trays. Brush with the reserved beaten egg. Bake in the middle of a hot oven, 220 degrees C/425 degrees F/Gas Mark 7, for about 10 minutes until just golden. Cool on a wire rack.

RECIPE

TOURNEDOS ROSSINI

*See page 48 for the explanation of the link between this
extravagant dish and Brighton.*

Ingredients

4 tournedos of fillet beef,
approx 2.5cm (1 inch) thick
4 slices of pate foie gras
1 tablespoon of butter
1 tablespoon of olive oil
2 sliced truffles (for those
who can afford it!) or
otherwise use mushrooms of
your choice

Madeira wine
Port
Brandy
Good beef or veal stock
4 slices of white bread,
without the crust, toasted, of
the same size as the meat
3 garlic cloves, finely sliced
Brown demi-glace sauce (see
below)

Melt the butter and the oil in a hot frying pan; season the tournedos
with salt and pepper and fry rapidly in the butter and oil to seal.

To make the brown demi-glace sauce: deglaze the pan in which the
meat was fried with three drops of port, two drops of brandy, two
drops of Madeira wine and 80ml (3 fluid ounces) of beef or veal stock.
Allow to reduce.

In another non-stick pan, rapidly fry the slices of pate, and place on
absorbent paper. Braise the truffles or mushrooms in a little butter
with a spoonful of Madeira wine; add the brown sauce and let it
simmer for approximately three minutes. Keep hot.

Place a slice of toasted bread on each serving plate. Cover each
slice with a tournedo, a slice of pate and truffles or mushrooms. Cover
each serving with the sauce, and serve immediately.

QUIZ ANSWERS

1. King's Road, the seafront road of west Brighton, is named after George IV, who opened it in 1822. It was part of the principal 'carriage drive' of the town, and as such was not surfaced with tarmac until 1910.

2. The Booth Museum holds a collection of over half a million insects, including butterflies. There is also a collection of most species of birds found in the British Isles, which was formed by the naturalist Edward Thomas Booth; the birds are displayed in model panoramas of their natural habitats.

3. The Royal Pavilion at Brighton. It was also disliked by the satirist Sydney Smith, who said that 'The dome of St Paul's must have come to Brighton and pupped'.

4. George IV's Italian chef, the great Careme, devised the recipe for Tournedos Rossini for the composer Gioacchino Rossini (1792-1868), who stayed at the Royal Pavilion over Christmas 1823.

5. The young Laurence Olivier made his entrance and then fell flat on his face, to the delight of the audience, but presumably to his great embarrassment.

6. Lewis Carroll (real name Charles Dodgson) visited Brighton many times, as his sister lived at 11 Sussex Square from 1874 until 1887. The tunnel in the private gardens of the square is said to have been the inspiration for the opening chapter of 'Alice's Adventures in Wonderland'.

7. On the wall of the Brighthelm Community Centre in North Road. This attractive sculpture illustrating the Loaves and Fishes parable was created by Eric Gill.

8. In the year 2000 the unitary authority of Brighton & Hove was granted city status as part of the Millennium celebrations.

9. People from the Brighton & Hove community come to 'Seedy Sunday' to swap organically-grown seeds and listen to talks on seeds. Most of the seeds being swapped will be adapted to local conditions and will therefore be able to grow well. The idea behind the scheme is that the process of seed-swapping leads to the building up of a wide variety in the crops being grown locally, which is most important in preserving biodiversity. Many crop varieties have become extinct since the onset of industrial agriculture, and it is most important that the existing heritage varieties are grown in as wide an area as possible.

10. Residents of Hove have traditionally seen their town as a separate area from Brighton, and it is often referred to by locals as 'Hove actually'. This came about because the question 'Do you live in Brighton?' is often answered with the response 'No, Hove actually!'. The Station pub at Hove was once known as 'Bertie Belcher's Brighton Brewery Company at the Hedgehog and Hogshead - it's really in Hove, actually!'.

BRIGHTON, THE CHAIN PIER 1880 B2085017

BRIGHTON, THE BEACH 1898 41890

FRANCIS FRITH

PIONEER VICTORIAN PHOTOGRAPHER

Francis Frith, founder of the world-famous photographic archive, was a complex and multi-talented man. A devout Quaker and a highly successful Victorian businessman, he was philosophical by nature and pioneering in outlook. By 1855 he had already established a wholesale grocery business in Liverpool, and sold it for the astonishing sum of £200,000, which is the equivalent today of over £15,000,000. Now in his thirties, and captivated by the new science of photography, Frith set out on a series of pioneering journeys up the Nile and to the Near East.

INTRIGUE AND EXPLORATION

He was the first photographer to venture beyond the sixth cataract of the Nile. Africa was still the mysterious 'Dark Continent', and Stanley and Livingstone's historic meeting was a decade into the future. The conditions for picture taking confound belief. He laboured for hours in his wicker dark-room in the sweltering heat of the desert, while the volatile chemicals fizzed dangerously in their trays. Back in London he exhibited his photographs and was 'rapturously cheered' by members of the Royal Society. His reputation as a photographer was made overnight.

VENTURE OF A LIFE-TIME

By the 1870s the railways had threaded their way across the country, and Bank Holidays and half-day Saturdays had been made obligatory by Act of Parliament. All of a sudden the working man and his family were able to enjoy days out, take holidays, and see a little more of the world.

With typical business acumen, Francis Frith foresaw that these new tourists would enjoy having souvenirs to commemorate their days out. For the next thirty years he travelled the country by train and by pony and trap, producing fine photographs of seaside resorts and beauty spots that were keenly bought by millions of Victorians. These prints were painstakingly pasted into family albums and pored over during the dark nights of winter, rekindling precious memories of summer excursions. Frith's studio was soon supplying retail shops all over the country, and by 1890 F Frith & Co had become the greatest specialist photographic publishing company in the world, with over 2,000 sales outlets, and pioneered the picture postcard.

FRANCIS FRITH'S LEGACY

Francis Frith had died in 1898 at his villa in Cannes, his great project still growing. By 1970 the archive he created contained over a third of a million pictures showing 7,000 British towns and villages.

Frith's legacy to us today is of immense significance and value, for the magnificent archive of evocative photographs he created provides a unique record of change in the cities, towns and villages throughout Britain over a century and more. Frith and his fellow studio photographers revisited locations many times down the years to update their views, compiling for us an enthralling and colourful pageant of British life and character.

We are fortunate that Frith was dedicated to recording the minutiae of everyday life. For it is this sheer wealth of visual data, the painstaking chronicle of changes in dress, transport, street layouts, buildings, housing and landscape that captivates us so much today, offering us a powerful link with the past and with the lives of our ancestors.

Computers have now made it possible for Frith's many thousands of images to be accessed almost instantly. The archive offers every one of us an opportunity to examine the places where we and our families have lived and worked down the years. Its images, depicting our shared past, are now bringing pleasure and enlightenment to millions around the world a century and more after his death.

For further information visit: www.francisfrith.com

INTERIOR DECORATION

Frith's photographs can be seen framed and as giant wall murals in thousands of pubs, restaurants, hotels, banks, retail stores and other public buildings throughout Britain. These provide interesting and attractive décor, generating strong local interest and acting as a powerful reminder of gentler days in our increasingly busy and frenetic world.

FRITH PRODUCTS

All Frith photographs are available as prints and posters in a variety of different sizes and styles. In the UK we also offer a range of other gift and stationery products illustrated with Frith photographs, although many of these are not available for delivery outside the UK – see our web site for more information on the products available for delivery in your country.

THE INTERNET

Over 100,000 photographs of Britain can be viewed and purchased on the Frith web site. The web site also includes memories and reminiscences contributed by our customers, who have personal knowledge of localities and of the people and properties depicted in Frith photographs. If you wish to learn more about a specific town or village you may find these reminiscences fascinating to browse. Why not add your own comments if you think they would be of interest to others? See **www.francisfrith.com**

PLEASE HELP US BRING FRITH'S PHOTOGRAPHS TO LIFE

Our authors do their best to recount the history of the places they write about. They give insights into how particular towns and villages developed, they describe the architecture of streets and buildings, and they discuss the lives of famous people who lived there. But however knowledgeable our authors are, the story they tell is necessarily incomplete.

Frith's photographs are so much more than plain historical documents. They are living proofs of the flow of human life down the generations. They show real people at real moments in history; and each of those people is the son or daughter of someone, the brother or sister, aunt or uncle, grandfather or grandmother of someone else. All of them lived, worked and played in the streets depicted in Frith's photographs.

We would be grateful if you would give us your insights into the places shown in our photographs: the streets and buildings, the shops, businesses and industries. Post your memories of life in those streets on the Frith website: what it was like growing up there, who ran the local shop and what shopping was like years ago; if your workplace is shown tell us about your working day and what the building is used for now. Read other visitors' memories and reconnect with your shared local history and heritage. With your help more and more Frith photographs can be brought to life, and vital memories preserved for posterity, and for the benefit of historians in the future.

Wherever possible, we will try to include some of your comments in future editions of our books. Moreover, if you spot errors in dates, titles or other facts, please let us know, because our archive records are not always completely accurate—they rely on 140 years of human endeavour and hand-compiled records. You can email us using the contact form on the website.

Thank you!

For further information, trade, or author enquiries
please contact us at the address below:

**The Francis Frith Collection, 6 Oakley Business Park,
Dinton, Salisbury, Wiltshire, England SP3 5EU.**
Tel: +44 (0)1722 716 376 Fax: +44 (0)1722 716 881
e-mail: sales@francisfrith.co.uk **www.francisfrith.com**